Essentialism in Business For Beginners:

Determine Essential Things in Your Business and Get Rid of Things That Waste Your Time and Money

By

Dale Blake

Table of Contents

Chapter 1. Setting the Mood: A Correct Mind Set................ 5

Chapter 2. Essential Startup Steps... 9

Chapter 3. Some Theories in Business................................ 16

Chapter 4. Business Structure and Management 18

Chapter 5. Major Business Flops... 21

Final Words 27

Thank You Page 28

Essentialism in Business For Beginners: Determine Essential Things in Your Business and Get Rid of Things That Waste Your Time and Money

By Dale Blake

© Copyright 2014 Dale Blake

Reproduction or translation of any part of this work beyond that permitted by section 107 or 108 of the 1976 United States Copyright Act without permission of the copyright owner is unlawful. Requests for permission or further information should be addressed to the author.

This publication is designed to provide accurate and authoritative information in regard to the subject matter covered. This work is sold with the understanding that the publisher is not engaged in rendering legal, accounting, or other professional services. If legal advice or other expert assistance is required, the services of a competent professional person should be sought.

First Published, 2014

Printed in the United States of America

Chapter 1. Setting the Mood: A Correct Mind Set

Starting a business is a challenge for beginners. Be it a small or a big one, you have to have passion, enthusiasm and knowledge in order to succeed in it. Aside from endowing yourself with these, it is also important to equip yourself with an attitude of a risk taker, who knows how to make calculated risks, as any business enthusiast would say, a business is a wager that yields to either you winning or losing the game. If you are planning to put up a business, it is imperative to understand that doing so demands a lot of things to the business owner, the proprietor or the entrepreneur. As the key player in the game, the business owner is in charge of a number of responsibilities from the planning stage, implementation stage and even beyond it when sustaining it becomes the concern. The idea of starting your own business is similar to any other beginnings such as finishing a college degree or building your own career. What resembles these to a business is the initial requirement each demands, that is, motivation.

The initial requirement in putting up a business is the presence of motivation or drive that emanates from the business owner himself or herself. In other words, if you have no interest at all to push through with it despite having the means, the business, prima facie, is certainly bound to fail. Therefore, as the business owner, you should have the spirit to carry out the responsibilities of the key player who is ready to take the challenges of a risk taker, further have the drive to sustain that spirit. In order to do so, it is important to choose the right kind of business you engage in. Putting up a business goes with choosing a kind of business within your area of interest or that which you are good at. If you are interested in cooking, a restaurant might be a good business for you and a better avenue to further develop your cooking skills; if you are fond of fashion like clothes, shoes, and the like, a boutique might be a good choice to pick for your business, a delight to your fashionable personality. If photography interests you, a studio business is apt for you. It doesn't matter if you are starting big or small, a small food stand, a stall of a selection of toys, a buy and sell business, a real estate endeavour, as long as you have the drive to start a business which you are interested at, then you are on the right track.

This primary consideration will jumpstart a potential successful business. But what else need to be considered? In a typical scenario, a *newbie* in business has a lot of things in mind. A mish mash of ideas and questions on what type of business to build, how big (or small) should the business be, how many employees to hire, how much to pay for each, how much initial capital to produce, and such other concerns that lead one to nowhere or a scattered beginning. Because of this, the tendency is to consult other people who can help you keep track of your goals, a friend who is into business, an expert who can educate you on the theories of business or maybe a financial adviser. However, while this may help, you have to be able to figure out if it is necessary to consult such. Ironically, when you know how to keep your goals intact and your drive on fire, you will reach the finish line without having to spend money to pay a financial adviser just yet. In fact, what you have to equip yourself with is the proper knowledge to start and sustain a successful business. First, be clear with your answers to questions that matter most in starting a business. "What other concerns should I focus on?" Second, as you are set to dive into a business career, with the correct mind set, believing that you can, what comes next? Be ready to learn more. Feed your mind with the appropriate knowledge in business. Familiarize yourself with the checklist of business essentials.

Chapter 2. Essential Startup Steps

Know thyself: The Role of the Captain

"Knowledge is power." In completing the business plan, you have a readily available tool to examine your goals, tasks accomplished and things that need to be done. But starting a business does not end here. It requires a cyclical process of learning, relearning and unlearning. As you discover along the way or in the process your strengths, weaknesses, opportunities and threats, you become more aware of your capabilities as an entrepreneur. Knowing your responsibilities is fundamental in business. At the outset, responsibilities should be clear, but in the process of carrying them out, they thrive. Be aware of these obligations and keep them in mind by being innovative and flexible as you run your business.

The following are the common duties of an entrepreneur, a businessman or businesswoman or a proprietor:
To do a research on the business.
To analyze the industry.

To plan the execution of the business plan.

To manage the affairs of the business.

To represent and build networks in order to sustain the business.

Getting things done

For a beginner, being organized is one major key to consider. Thus, to follow the essential steps of putting up a business may be necessary, learning from the experiences of those who have been there, starting small and becoming big through time. While it may not be manageable in the beginning, you will surely get through as you grasp the hang of it. As you start small, keep in mind the following essential startup steps:

Do Your Research

Researching is indispensable in starting a business. It will enable you to know your market, particularly the customers, the competitors and the industry in general. Through this, you become aware of the most appropriate products or services to offer to the existing market. The process of research may not be as tedious in the strict sense of the concept, but it could be any process that will certainly encompass your target, that is, to be familiar with the three major concerns: customers, competitors and industry. As you engage and complete the research process, the results of which will give your business a direction and ensure that you are on top of what your customers are after. Having considered all these will help you concretize the first essential startup step, a business plan.

"Think it through": Build a business plan

The business plan serves as the backbone of your business. It allows you to gain, if not deepen your understanding of your industry structure, competitive landscape and the capital requirement for a business neophyte. A result of a study conducted to know the effectiveness of a business plan for beginners states that companies with a business plan have 50% more profits and revenue than non-planning businesses. Through a business plan, you will easily crystallize your goals as it is premised on a framework of essentials. As the skeleton of your business, it should be comprehensive possessing the following components:

Business Overview

The business overview contains an introduction of what your business is all about. Discuss in your overview your business choice, the significance of your business. It is basically a presentation of what the business is all about in a nutshell.

Products or services

Present in this component the products or services you are going to offer to your customers by laying down the particular or exact details of what you are going to sell (for products) or provide (for services) and how it will be produced. Moreover, be able to identify an appropriate branding and packaging that will give identity to your business. Show your products or services' special features capitalizing on the distinct feature/s vis-à-vis other competitors' features. Worthy of discussion in this aspect of the business plan is the price or price range you intend to accord to your products or services. In price allocation, it is required that you consider the costs, labor and other overheads for a more reasonable gain, without putting at risk the quality of the products or services.

Market Analysis

Further research might be of help in supplying contents for this component. The industry that you choose to delve in needs to be studied further, in order for your business to survive in such environment. You have to be able to identify what market your products or services will serve and why. If you are to put up a boutique for fashion, you have to critically analyze the innovations and trends in fashion, competitors' strategies and most importantly, how to fill a viable gap which will fit your business in the arena of fashion boutiques. Make sure that as you do market analysis, you include details such as 1) people who will purchase your products, 2) location of your business, 3) state of the market (growing, declining or segmented), 4) market influences, 5) business price range (high, low or middle).

Competition

One thing that you should not miss considering is the competition in the market. You can either take it as an opportunity or threat. Either way, you have to learn to survive the competition, otherwise, you lose the chance to make a name in the business field. As you research, make a profiling of your competitors by basically identifying who or what they are, how you position your product or service against them, the competitive edge of your business, its benefits to the customers vis-à-vis theirs underscoring the comparison of prices. If competition is tight, evident on the quantity of competitors, take advantage of providing a relatively lower price that will encourage customers to patronize you more instead of other competitors. How good you play along with the competition present in the market gives you a vantage point to stand out in the business you have chosen.

Marketing Strategy: Decide on a Business Name
Opportunities don't happen. You create them. Grab the opportunity to create your own and original branding for your business, this is the so-called marketing strategy. For a beginner, how you promote your products or services is very crucial. Remember, you are starting from scratch, thus, your market strategy matters a lot. Identify how, when and where you intend to promote your business. Will it be in a form of online advertising, printed materials, flyers or leaflets? As you embark on the business, plan the

details of your launching and include it in your marketing strategy. Moreover, thinking of a unique and remarkable brand, that which attracts customers or clients, may contribute to a better position for your business in the playing field. Thinking of what is best for your business in any facet always leads you back to your customers. Your creativity will help you think of the most appropriate marking stategy/ies for your business.

Analysis of the strengths and weaknesses, opportunities and threats will help you to determine the right goals for your business.

The marketing strategy an entrepreneur chooses may serve as its flagship which can potentially give name to the business in the industry. Strategies are grounded on particular theories in business. Worthy to know are the theories from which these strategies are derived that one can use to come up with the right, timely and smart one for his business.

Chapter 3. Some Theories in Business

One business author suggests how one should apply successful case studies to one's life. Relevant to business, handling one demands banking on different approaches and theories. The successful businessmen or entrepreneurs certainly have particular backbone theories from which their businesses bank on.

Theory 1: Principal Agent or Incentive Theory
Incentives can be a significant factor for people to work harder. A research study posits that people work as hard as they are paid. Also, a business may foster if incentives are awarded to customers like providing discounts for students, giving perks to regular customers and the like. You can embark on this marketing strategy to build a name, sustain a robust clientele without jeopardizing the incentives your employees should equally receive.

Theory 2: Disruptive Innovation Theory
This theory purports that weak and small, but more innovative businesses have a great chance to overtake their competitors.

This statement means that it is okay to start small. If starting small means eventually multiplying, then it is a good sign of a successful business. The disruptive theory encourages the marketing strategy of multiplying into small businesses innovatively. You can begin with a simple step of starting small and equipping yourself and your business with an innovate marketing strategy. Before you know it, you are on top of your competitors.

Chapter 4. Business Structure and Management

A business, just like any other organization, should subscribe to a particular structure. Classify your business as sole trader (for sole proprietorship), partnership (for two ownerships) or company (with multiple ownerships). The structure for your business speaks of the business' organization. You are able to show a chain of responsibility through its structure. It also aids in the systematic functioning of the business particularly managing the people. Identify the key roles of all the people from the highest level of the hierarchy, the middle managers and other members of the team, for companies or big businesses. For small businesses, which require a minimal number of employees, how each operates and functions should also be discussed in this component. Showing the relationship of one from the other, particularly showing the proper protocol, will not only ensure a responsible work ethics but of a proper management of time, effort and other resources.

Finances or Business Budget

Money is an essential commodity that helps you run your business. Most businesses require stable finances to jumpstart them. In rare occasions, no capital is required. But the indispensability of finances should be given careful attention in the business plan both for small and big businesses. Identify the costs you will be incurring as you start your business. In fact, do so upon the initial step of planning to come up with one. In other words, the business budget is needed to start and operate a business from its conception to the day the business begins to generate profit. Know how you will finance your business. Do you intend to loan capital for it? Will it come from your personal fund or investment capital? How much of what you have are you willing to risk for your business?

Lay down all other costings that cover start-up costs (rent and facilities, utilities, supplies and equipment, equipment maintenance, legal compliance and marketing and promotion) , salary and fixed overheads, and also your financial projections including how much you need to break even, when you are likely to make profit or growth expectations.

Your Action Plan

This is the most important component of your business plan. It contains how you are going to achieve your goals identified in the earlier part of the plan. Included in the action plan are:

Objectives (reiterate your goals),

Key tasks to be done,

Persons in charge of the tasks, and

Time frame.

Make sure that your objectives comply with the SMART formula as any other task considers, namely, Specific, Measurable, Attainable, Relevant and Time bound. If you don't achieve a task, reschedule it, in case it is still not done by the second date, ask why. Is it too large? Is it unclear how it will help the business? Do you have the skills to do it? Be able to carefully review your action plan from time to time for this will surely help you modify plans if necessary.

Chapter 5. Major Business Flops

The aforesaid discussions are key factors in starting a business. To consider them in preparing and planning for your business will yield to a potential success of your business. However, it is a common scenario that as one engages himself or herself in something foreign like putting up a business, mistakes are unintentionally (or maybe intentionally) committed brought about by poor knowledge and/or poor planning. In starting a business, there are several identified common mistakes one commits. As they are common, it will certainly help to learn about them early on so that overcoming them will not be a problem because you foresee avoiding them, or in case you have been trapped by these common flops, you might still consider finding a way to surpass them eventually.

Failing to make a business plan. This proves the business delusional. You have concepts in mind about the business. But having the idea is one thing, writing it is another. Unless the business plan is in black and white, realizing a business is near to impossible. While the business plan is not an indicator of a business' success, as mentioned in the beginning, it serves as a blueprint in jumpstarting any business endeavor. Those who tend to skip this essential requisite of business tend to evade the demand of making a business plan. Indeed it is time consuming and demanding in terms of research work, but investing time and effort in coming up with one will also save you so much in the future. Therefore, never fail to make a business plan.

Taking your eye off the competition. The business plan requires the identification of competitors in the workplace you choose to compete at. But a common mistake to many is ignoring the competition. This could mean failing to address the marketability of your products or services by looking at the existing businesses similar to that which you plan to offer, which proves relevant and essential in business. Moreover, it is also common in this aspect the failure to understand market saturation. This is the maximum sales volume for a product or service under current market conditions assuming a constant level of demand. For example, if in your chosen work environment in a 'small' community there are a number of business establishments on beauty salon from which you derive the idea of a good competition thus deciding to put up a similar business, you might have failed to consider the market saturation in your locale. Make sure that as you engage in business, you consider how it will take part in a healthy competitive environment while also considering the quantity of the clientele your business and other competitors shall serve.

Weak financial planning. Being financially prepared has a big share in the pie of startup essentials. The business plan also requires that you identify the source of your finances. Your financial capacity should be able to address both preliminary and future costs of the business. However, most people who engage in business tend to prepare only for the preliminary costs failing to prepare for a financial contingency plan. When faced with situations beyond your control, it is important that you are prepared to deal with it, thus, a contingency plan which serves as your safety net. For this particular concern, it may be beneficial to consider asking for a professional advice to help you in deciding financial concerns of your business. Moreover, some expert opinions claim that resorting to loans from families and friends may be catastrophic especially to personal relationships with them. If borrowing money is an option to finance your business, receive loans from institutions that specialize on this matter.

Expecting immediate return of investment (ROI). "New businesses usually take two years to become profitable." Ninety-five percent of businesses will not make money when they first open and a large proportion of new businesses will not make significant money for years. During the seeding period of the business, expect that there will be more money to spend than to save. This is a typical undertaking of a business. It is thus ambitious to anticipate an immediate return of investment, except on rare occasion when luck is on your side. It is understandable if the business does not gain profit instantly as any business goes through the birthing stage with more loss than gain, or no gain at all. Do not be discouraged if you experience this, remember, "No pain, no gain."

Doing everything alone. No man is an island. If you try to do everything without the help of other, even if you claim it is just a small business or one-person business, you will definitely find difficulty surviving the demands of the business. The reality is, no matter how small or big your business may be there are various tasks that need to be done which requires a number of people to do them. Doing everything alone will not save money or effort, if that's what you think. It will rather cause more peril and instability in your business because you are jeopardizing the quality of the job if you try to do all things independently. Make sure, however, that when you decide to ask help from others, you choose the right people. Another common mistake one commits relevant to this misnomer is to employ people who are not appropriate for the jobs. The success of the new business is also determined by the quality of people you employ. Have a clear standard and requirements so you will not go wrong choosing only the right partners in your business.

Relying on verbal agreements. Putting all agreements in paper gives you and your business a sense of security. Do not just be contented with verbal agreements that may be easily tarnished. Even if it is just a simple agreement of getting things done, or a complicated contract, whether you personally know the person or your business partner, put everything in writing. This is important for any legal undertaking or for any future references. It is better to be safe than sorry. Learn to develop the habit of documenting everything as your business security blanket.

Doing ONLY what you love. While it is true that your business choice must be within your sphere of interest, it is also a misconception that you should only engage in the kind of business that you love. It is not a guarantee though that when you do the business that interests you success in the business follows, that is only one side of the story. The rest lies upon how you work on making it successful. Paradoxically, you can also contract in a business that may not be within the periphery of what you interest. In fact, one expert opinion claims that "there's a whole lot of people out there who love things they're not good at." In reality, if you do what you are good at or possess a driving spirit in something whether it is your interest or not, you can get going.

Final Words

Making the bold decision to start a new business is challenging. But as soon as you have decided to do so, you have to be prepared to equip yourself with the right knowledge and right attitude. The point is to build a strong foundation that will guard you as you engage in the nitty-gritty of starting your own business. Success may not come immediately or may not come at all, but be true to your goals and religiously respond to them while also carrying out the key roles of the captain of the ship. As the entrepreneur whose tasks include researching, analyzing, planning, implementing and sustaining the business, you can make a difference if you keep the drive and motivation to reach your goals. Starting a business may be difficult, but as soon as you are ready, free from the qualms and apprehensions, free from the pitfalls of poor planning, you will succeed.

Thank You Page

I want to personally thank you for reading my book. I hope you found information in this book useful and I would be very grateful if you could leave your honest review about this book. I certainly want to thank you in advance for doing this.

www.ingramcontent.com/pod-product-compliance
Lightning Source LLC
LaVergne TN
LVHW021748060526
838200LV00052B/3536